1

ISBN:979-8-9990779-1-2

This book is intended as a practical resource and informational guide. It is not a substitute for professional counseling or therapy. The author and publisher assume no liability for outcomes related to the use of this book.

THE FIRE THAT CONSUMES NOTHING

Living After the Self Dissolves

by

Ethan Starke

INTRODUCTION

(The Scorched Earth)

There was a time I lost everything —
not just what I had, but who I was.
The collapse was not poetic.
It didn't feel like a spiritual shedding or the beginning
of a journey.
It felt like death.

I stood inside the heat of that ruin —
surrounded by smoke, by the stench of what had
burned.
There was no relief. No clarity. No voice from within.
Just absence. And silence.
And the ache of having nothing to return to.

My thoughts tried to find a foothold:
*Where do I start? What can I salvage? What should I
fix?*
But the answer kept rising like a stone:
You can't. It's all gone.

This wasn't metaphor.
This wasn't symbolic transformation.
It was real — material, emotional, relational, spiritual
disintegration.
Everything that once held shape — home, purpose,

identity, love, even belief —
was gone.

And I didn't feel strong.
I didn't feel initiated or awakened.
I felt erased.

The language of healing did not apply here.
There was nothing left to heal — because there was
nothing left.
Only the scorched ground beneath my feet, and the
unbearable knowledge
that nothing I once held
was coming back.

This is not the space this book is about —
but it is the space this book comes from.

Every silence described in the pages to come
was born in the fire that left me hollow.

There is no true disappearance without burning.
There is no spaciousness without devastation.
There is no peace without the death of the one who
clung to it.

(From Salvage to Surrender)

There comes a moment — not always loud, not
always conscious —
when something in you stops reaching for the broken

pieces.
The questions slow.
The reflex to fix, to explain, to recover… fades.
Not because it's resolved, but because it no longer
makes sense to pretend.

I stood in the ruin for a long time trying to salvage
what I could.
A name. A story. A version of myself that might
survive this collapse.
But it became clear — brutally, finally —
that there was nothing left to save.

And in that recognition,
something softened.

Not relief. Not grace.
But a kind of quiet refusal to continue the
performance.

I didn't rise.
I didn't rebuild.
I simply stopped moving.

The mind kept trying —
whispering: *You need a new identity. A new plan. A
new reason.*
But those thoughts began to pass like ghosts —
lacking weight, lacking invitation.

The stillness that arrived wasn't chosen.
It wasn't sought or earned.

It was what remained when the one who always
moved… no longer could.

And in that stillness,
the question *"What now?"* disappeared.

There was no "now" to answer.
No one left to lead the search.
No destination waiting in the wings.

This is the turning.

It is not a decision.
It is a recognition —
that the world you were holding was already gone,
and that there is a kind of life on the other side of
effort
that cannot be imagined
until effort itself collapses.

The fire does not bring this.
The fire only clears the illusion.

This…
this is what's left
when you stop looking for yourself
in what has burned.

At first, it felt like absence.
No identity to inhabit. No role to return to.
I wasn't becoming anything. I wasn't even recovering.
I was just… here.

The silence didn't feel sacred.
It felt hollow.
As if everything that once animated me had packed
up and left —
and somehow, I remained.

But I wasn't sure what remained.
I couldn't call it "me."
It had no name, no aim, no reaction.
It didn't strive. It didn't interpret. It didn't defend.

It simply witnessed.

There was a stillness that wasn't about peace.
It wasn't pleasant, or blissful, or even healing.
It was just *there* —
a space untouched by thought,
unmoved by praise or pain,
unconcerned with my survival as a person.

For the first time,
there was no one watching me.
No self to adjust.
No audience, even inwardly.
And in that vacancy,
there was no pressure to become anything.

That's when I realized:
This space is not the absence of self.
It's the absence of the need for self.

It was not a grand revelation.
It arrived like breath —
barely noticed, but always present.

The world continued.
People spoke to me as though I was still someone.
They asked me how I was doing, what I was planning,
what I wanted next.

I listened,
but I did not answer from the place they expected.

There was no answer.
Just a quiet presence watching everything unfold —
without reacting, without attaching,
without needing to prove that it was real.

And still, I did things.
I ate. I walked. I spoke. I lived.
But it no longer felt personal.
The doer was gone.
What remained was awareness moving through a body,
a selfless life flowing through form.

Not higher. Not lower.
Just *untethered.*

This space did not arrive fully formed.
It unfolded — not with clarity, but with subtraction.

At first, it was disorienting.
To live without the scaffolding of "me"
is to lose every shortcut the mind uses to define
reality.
But what emerged in its place was not confusion —
it was a series of quiet truths
that revealed themselves one layer at a time.

The first shift was simple, almost disappointing:
There's nothing actually holding me.

All the rules, the obligations, the inner pressure to
strive —
they weren't real.
They were inherited beliefs, assumed contracts,
invisible prisons.

I saw that I had been keeping myself bound
by ideas no one was enforcing.
The voices I thought were external
were echoes of my own fear.

And when I stopped agreeing with them —
they disappeared.

Then came a deeper seeing:
Me and *who I am* are not one and the same.
The self — the personality, the story, the identity — is
an accumulation.
It's a costume made of memory, culture, trauma, and
repetition.
But underneath it...
is something untouched.

Call it soul. Call it essence. Call it the witness.
It does not perform.
It does not defend.
It simply is.

And it is enough.

In that stillness, another layer burned away:
Why did we ever admire money, titles, status?

I saw that the admiration of material success
was not just a distraction — it was a kind of worship.
A drug.
One that kept people from turning toward the one
thing truly worthy of awe:

The Source itself.

God — not as an entity, but as the sacred, formless
root of all that is.
Unseen. Unowned. Beyond display.

The only thing worthy of reverence is the thing no one can ever possess.

Everything else is theater.

Next came the soft collapse of the spiritual ego.
The part of me that still wanted to "live my truth,"
"fulfill my potential," "achieve wholeness."

I saw the rules of that game too.
Be authentic. Be disciplined. Be radiant. Be unique.

And it all felt like school again.

A different uniform, but still a performance.

And then I realized:
You can live without those rules.
You can step out of the game entirely —
and life continues.
Quiet. Undramatic. Free.

But freedom didn't mean nihilism.
It meant choosing from clarity — not obligation.

In the quiet, I began to notice what still felt beautiful.
Honesty. Gentleness. Integrity. Silence.
Not because I was told to value them,
but because they felt true when everything else fell away.

There was no longer a moral code I had to live by.
But there was still an orientation —
like a compass made of something older than thought.

And so I chose to keep a few simple principles.
Not because I must.
But because they made sense
in the presence of what I had seen.

And finally — the lightest, strangest, most liberating revelation:
It's all theater.

Life kept going. People kept playing their roles.
Money changed hands. Clothes were worn. Deadlines came and went.

But I wasn't *in* it anymore.
I was *with* it.
Like someone who knows they're in a play,
and decides to act anyway —
with joy, with presence, with flair —
but never again forgetting:
It isn't real.

So yes, I wear clothes. I speak languages. I pay bills.
Sometimes I even dress to impress.

But none of it touches who I am.
Because I'm not playing to win.
I'm playing because I can.

And that…
is freedom.

I live here.
I wake up, I speak, I laugh, I carry out the tasks of my day.
But I no longer belong to any of it.

Not because I've withdrawn —
but because I've stopped confusing participation with possession.

I don't own the moments I move through.
I don't inhabit a role called "myself."
I don't defend a position, or seek a title, or protect an image.

I simply witness.

It's not detachment.
It's intimacy without clinging.

I feel everything —
the joy, the sadness, the confusion of others, the ache of beauty, the rush of presence —
but I don't become what I feel.
I don't turn it into an identity.

The witness is not numb.
It is not passive.
It is alive — more alive than I ever was as a self.

15

Because now, nothing is personal.
And so everything is sacred.

The world still tries to name me.
To pull me back into the old game.

It hands me labels — success, failure, good, bad,
lovable, flawed.
It hands me numbers — income, age, likes, degrees.
It asks me to care.

And sometimes, I do.
Briefly. Playfully.
I wear the mask, I speak the language, I bow to the
ritual.

But underneath it all, I remain untouched.

There's a quiet joy in this way of living.
Like watching a play, knowing it's fiction,
and choosing to give your whole heart to it anyway.

Not because you believe it's real —
but because you see the beauty in *offering yourself
without needing anything in return.*

That is the difference.

I am no longer trying to win.
No longer trying to become.
No longer trying to last.

I am simply here —
without agenda, without ambition, without resistance.

And in that,
there is a fullness the world could never give me.

This is not a guide.
This is not a map.
There is no process here to follow, no promise to
reach, no method to trust.

This book will not take you anywhere.
Because there is nowhere to go.

There is only the seeing.
The clear, unsentimental seeing of what remains
when the noise fades,
when the identity falls away,
when the seeking stops.

And what remains —
is what has always been.

I'm not writing to teach.
I'm not writing to explain.
I'm writing because something in me is still dissolving,
and what's left has become so quiet, so spacious,
that words occasionally rise up like soft signals from
deep water.

Not to convince.
Not to fix.
Just to say:
You're not imagining this.

If you've begun to feel yourself falling out of the self,
if you've tasted the dissonance between who you
were and what remains —
if the world around you continues,
but the person you once were can no longer
reappear...

Then this book is not instruction.
It is recognition.

Each chapter is a mirror.
Each passage is a clearing.

They are not written for the mind that wants to grasp
—
but for the part of you that already knows,
the part that remembers the freedom
that comes not from becoming,
but from no longer needing to be.

And if, somewhere along the way, the words
disappear,
and you find yourself just sitting there,
breathing,
not thinking,

not striving,
just… here —

Then the book has already done what it came to do.

Because beyond all of this —
beyond the fire, the silence, the stages, the witness —
what remains
is not a state.

It is the end of the one who seeks.

And what is left
needs nothing
to be whole.

Craving — The Ache for More

There is a fire that burns quietly inside us —
the fire of craving.
Not desire for one thing or another,
but the ache that lies beneath all wanting:
the ache to become.

From childhood, it begins.
Be better. Be worthy. Be loved. Be enough.
The flame is lit before we even know we're alive.
And from that moment on, we run.

We chase knowledge. We chase beauty.
We chase improvement, safety, reputation,
transcendence.
We chase versions of ourselves —
stronger, calmer, more enlightened, more admired —
never seeing that the chase itself is the continuation
of suffering.

Craving is not about what we want.
It's about **who we think we'll be when we get it.**

At its root, craving is identity.
It is the belief that we are **not yet**.
That there is something missing, and that the missing
thing will complete us.

That if we can just reach it — the relationship, the recognition, the inner peace —
we will finally get to rest.

But there is no rest for the one who craves.
Because the very self that is built by craving
can only exist *as long as the hunger continues.*

The moment you stop needing more,
the self begins to dissolve.

And so it fights.
It fuels the next longing.
The next goal.
The next spiritual badge.

Even the desire to be free
can become its mask.

There is, perhaps, no craving more subtle
than the craving to be *good.*

To be wise.
To be kind.
To be seen as loving, conscious, awakened, clear.

This form of craving is harder to detect —
because it wears the language of virtue.
But it too is a strategy.
A performance.

The self rebrands itself as a seeker of truth,
 but it is still seeking safety, worth, and belonging —
 only now, through moral identity.

It says: *I am not okay as I am. But if I am good
enough — conscious enough —*
 *then I'll finally be safe from judgment, chaos, and
loss.*

But no amount of goodness can make the self real.
 Because it was never under threat to begin with.
 Only the illusion believed otherwise.

There is a difference between **natural desire** and
craving.
 Desire is part of life — the body hungers, the heart
reaches, the soul moves.
 These are not the problem.

The problem is when the *self* hijacks the movement
—

 when desire becomes identity,
 when we want not just the thing,
 but the *meaning* it will give us.

A flower opens to the sun. It is not craving.
 But we chase light in order to feel significant.

That's the fire:
 not the wanting itself,
 but the belief that we *are* what we want.

I didn't see this at first.
 I believed in the ache.
 I made it sacred.
 I called it purpose, or passion, or ambition, or even growth.
 And I followed it like a guide.

But no matter what I reached,
 the hunger remained.
 It simply changed shape —
 more subtle, more spiritual, more disguised.

Eventually, I ran out of places to run.

And in that stillness, I saw the truth:
 It was never the world I was chasing.
 It was myself.

A version of me that felt finished.
 Whole.
 Permanent.
 Unshakeable.

And such a version does not exist.

This is the lie at the center of craving:
 that somewhere out there, you will arrive.

But arrival is a myth.
 Because the self that longs for arrival
 must always remain incomplete.
 If it arrives, it dies.
 And it knows this.

So it keeps the story going.

The next job.
 The next lover.
 The next insight.
 The next chapter of healing.

And every time you get close, it moves the horizon.

It says: *Almost. Just a little more. You're not quite there yet.*

And so the fire burns on.

Craving cannot be satisfied,
 because it is not a need —
 it is a *belief in lack.*

You can feed it forever,
 but as long as you believe in the story that says *"you are not yet,"*
 you will burn.

Not from the heat of desire —
 but from the effort to become someone real.

That effort is the fire.
 That belief is the fuel.

And until you let both go,
 you will live in longing
 and call it a life.

Aversion — The War Against What Is

We are trained to believe that peace comes from
shaping the world.
 We shape it through action, through boundaries,
through plans, through belief —
 but beneath it all is one simple instinct:
 resist what is not wanted.

Aversion is the second fire.
 It is the refusal of reality.
 The quiet, relentless effort to escape what already is.

This fire doesn't always burn hot.
 Sometimes it looks like subtle tension —
 an inner flinch when something is said,
 an invisible wince when something is lost.

Other times it is rage.
 Control.
 Rejection.
 A desperate need to erase, correct, fix, avoid.

But always, at its root,
 is the belief that what is *should not be.*

That life, as it is now,
is unacceptable.

That *you*, as you are now,
are unacceptable.

I once thought this tension was strength —
that my intolerance for pain or conflict or wrongness
was evidence of integrity.

But I've come to see that most of what I resisted
was not harmful — just unfamiliar.
Or unflattering.
Or unscripted.

And even when it *was* painful,
my resistance never brought peace.
It only delayed the seeing.

Because when you fight what already is,
you are not protecting yourself —
you are preserving the illusion of control.

But aversion does more than protect.
It builds a self.

Every time I said *"I would never accept that,"*
I wasn't just describing a boundary.
I was building a person.

A self defined by opposition:
 *the one who refuses, who knows better, who is not
like them.*

I told myself I was principled.
 But beneath the principles was a fear:
 that if I didn't resist, I would disappear.

And in a way, I was right.

Because when resistance stops,
 so does the one who needed to exist in contrast.

No enemy, no protector.
 No opposition, no identity.

When the resistance finally breaks,
 what's left is not defeat —
 but silence.

There is no more war to fight.
 Not because everything is healed,
 but because there is no longer a *you*
 who needs to win.

You stop running from pain
 because you no longer believe it says anything about
who you are.

You stop chasing perfection
 because you no longer need the world to mirror a
story about your worth.

You stop editing the moment
because the one who edits
has disappeared into the seeing.

And what follows
is not enlightenment —
but stillness.

Not joy,
but the absence of tension.

Not clarity,
but the end of the one demanding answers.

You notice your breath.
You feel the weight of your body.
You hear the sounds of the world — unfiltered,
unjudged.
And it no longer occurs to you that anything needs to
change.

There is nothing left to fix.
Nothing left to become.
Nothing left to push away.

And somehow, without effort,
that is enough.

Aversion says: *I must control this to be okay.*
But freedom says:
I am okay even when nothing is controlled.

Not because things feel good,
 but because feeling good is no longer the measure of
being.

To live without aversion
 is not to invite harm.
 It is simply to stop naming the moment
 as enemy.

And when the enemy is gone,
 so is the defender.

And what remains
 is not surrender.

It is the end
 of the one who resisted surrender
 in the first place.

Delusion — The Dream of the Self

There is no fire more convincing than the one you can't see.
 Delusion doesn't shout. It doesn't ache. It doesn't burn the skin.
 It simply *is*.
 A background hum. A lens so close to the eye, you forget it's there.

Delusion is the belief in a self that must be protected, defined, improved, explained.
 A self with a past and a future, with preferences and personality,
 with value and voice and vulnerability.
 A self who owns its story and believes it matters.

It is the belief:
 I am someone. And I must continue being that someone.

But look closely.
 The self changes with every situation.
 It contracts around threat.
 It expands around praise.
 It shifts with roles, with moods, with memory.

What you call "me"
is a story being edited in real time —
by fear, by habit, by social conditioning, by need.

And yet you hold to it
as if it were a single, solid thing.

That is delusion.

The mind says: *Of course I am someone. Look at my memories. Look at my feelings.*
But memories are interpretations.
And feelings are weather.
They pass.
They contradict.
They do not hold shape.

If you watch closely,
you'll see that everything you identify as self
is in motion.

And what moves
cannot be the thing that is watching.

The illusion of self doesn't only show up as ego or pride.
It shows up as the *roles you unconsciously perform*:

- The helper

- The fixer

- The strong one

- The misunderstood one

- The one who has been hurt but is still kind

- The one who speaks truth

- The one who always walks away

- The one who never gives up

These are not traits.
They are costumes.
And they are held in place by the belief that someone must be them.

Even pain can become identity.
Even resilience can become a mask.

Delusion doesn't care if the role is admirable.
Only that it *continues*.

But the most persistent mask —
the hardest one to see through —
is the *spiritual self.*

The one who knows.
The one who sees.
The one who's moved beyond.

It speaks slowly. It listens generously.
It offers soft truths. It posts wise things.
It calls itself awakened.

But it is still trying.
Still guarding a center.
Still performing goodness, wisdom, humility, or insight —
as if presence needs a personality.

And so the self reappears,
wearing silence like a badge.
Wearing surrender like a crown.

I clung to that version of me for a while.
The one who had let go.
The one who understood.

But even that was a performance.
An attempt to make non-being feel *important.*

Eventually, even that had to burn.
Even the witness had to dissolve.

Until there was nothing left but this:
awareness, unclaimed.

No role. No history. No future.

Not a new identity —
just the absence of one.

To lose the belief in self
 is not to become nothing.
 It is to stop pretending you were ever something.

What remains is not a person.
 It is not a soul.
 It is not a presence that can be captured or
described.

It is just this:
 aware, silent, clear.

And it needs no name.

The Myth of Becoming

At the center of striving is a simple idea:
 You are not yet.

It sounds harmless — even inspiring.
 You can grow. You can change. You can become
your highest self.

But this idea is a cage.
 Because as long as you are not yet,
 you are *never now.*

Becoming is the myth that says:
 There's a better version of you on the horizon —
 a version more healed, more successful, more
worthy, more loved.

And if you work hard enough,
 if you align your life just right,
 you'll finally catch up to the person you're supposed
to be.

But that person does not exist.

They are the horizon itself —
 forever appearing,
 never arriving.

I spent years believing in progress.
Not just in the outer world, but within.
Each new insight, each surrender, each tear, each
letting go —
I treated them like steps up a ladder I couldn't see
the top of.

Even in silence, I measured my stillness.
Even in surrender, I clung to the role of the one who
surrenders well.
Even in love, I searched for evidence that I was
evolving.

And it never stopped.
Because the self that believes in becoming
needs you to stay unfinished.

This myth is what keeps the fire alive.
It burns through ambition, through healing, through
identity.
It turns everything into fuel — even the parts of you
that long for rest.

Because rest would mean *stopping*.
And stopping would mean facing the truth:
That you are already here.
And there is no "more" to become.

But the mind resists this.
It says: *If I stop becoming, I will disappear. I will fall behind. I will waste this life.*

But that's just the voice of a system that needs movement to feel real.
And that voice isn't you.
It's the echo of a culture that worships change, progress, and image.

That voice believes that stillness is death.
Because in stillness, the one who was always becoming… vanishes.

And what remains
needs nothing to validate its being.

When the myth finally broke,
I didn't feel enlightened.
I didn't feel empowered.
I felt **empty**.

Not lost —
but no longer arriving.

Not finished —
but no longer defined.

I stopped trying to be anything.
And something deeper than identity
started to live through me.

Not as "me,"
but as life itself —
unlabeled, unmeasured, unclaimed.

You were never on a path.
There was never a finish line.
There is no prize for becoming.

There is only this moment,
and the quiet invitation to stop running.

Not to give up.
But to see clearly:

You were never missing.
You were never improving.
You were only remembering —
and forgetting —
and remembering again
that you have always been
what you already are.

Interlude: The Arrival

For forty years, I carried a self I didn't choose.
It wore my name, but it wasn't mine.
Its shape was sculpted by other people's stories,
by expectations, accidents, trauma, and repetition.
Some layers I built to survive.
Some were given to me like uniforms I never took off.
And I wore them — until they became the only thing I
knew how to be.

Then came the fire.
Not a metaphor.
A real collapse — a purge so total it stripped away
everything I thought I was.
What looked like disaster turned out to be mercy.

At first, I resisted.
I tried to patch it back together.
I told myself: *I can fix this. I can rebuild.*
But there was nothing left to rebuild from.
No job. No structure. No applause. No safety net.

And then came the quiet.

It didn't arrive as peace.
It arrived as **absence**.
No more scaffolding. No more performance. No one
to be.

And somehow, in that emptiness,
 I felt something that had never come to me through
any form of success:
 freedom.

Like a prisoner stepping into the sunlight —
 blinking, thin, disoriented,
 but finally breathing.

Soon after, I joined a meditation retreat in Big Bear,
California —
 my first with Or HaLev.
 I came to deepen the quiet.
 To listen.
 To see if the silence had anything to say.

After checking in and dropping my bag in the room,
 I still had some light left in the day.
 So I wandered into the woods behind my cabin.

There, I found a path —
 old tire tracks, long reclaimed by the land.
 They led deeper into the forest,
 like an invitation to a place humans no longer
remembered.

I followed.

And then —
 in a small clearing between tall, ancient pines —
 it happened.

One tree.
 One beam of golden light.
 One single bird call.
 A breeze so soft it barely touched the air.

And suddenly,
 everything collapsed — not violently, but completely.

Time folded.
 My brain flooded with memory —
 of a place I hadn't been since childhood,
 a scent I had forgotten,
 a clarity I had never understood until now.

I didn't *see* these things.
 I *was* them.
 And in the middle of it,
 a message arrived.
 Not a voice. Not a vision. Just a knowing:
 You have arrived.

I fell to my knees,
 and I wept —
 from somewhere so deep there was no self left to
 hold it.

In that moment,
 I understood that my life had never been a series of
 scattered events.
 It had been a journey —
 one arc, one unfolding,
 crafted not by accident,
 but by something far larger than my plans.

The highs, the achievements, the losses, the
humiliations —
  none of them were detours.
  They were necessary.
  Every layer that was built
  had to burn.
  So I could finally see what was never built at all.

That what I am —
  without titles, roles, relationships, or story —
  is not *someone new.*

It is **no one**.

And in that no one,
  I touched the divine.

Not a god made in my image,
  but the Source beyond name,
  the stillness from which all things rise and return.

There was no fear.
  No agenda.
  No goal.

Just this:
  I am no one.
  I am no body.
  And that is enough.

Part II: Extinguishing

There is a moment when the burning ends.
Not because you've mastered it.
Not because you've conquered desire or conquered
the self.
But because there's nothing left to fuel the fire.

No more meaning to assign.
No more identity to protect.
No more truth to chase.

Just silence.
Heavy at first.
Then light.
Then transparent.

This part of the book is not about revelation.
It is about disappearance.

Not the loss of life,
but the end of the one who needed life to be anything.

The seeker doesn't die all at once.
It fades.
It stops returning.
It becomes unnecessary.

And what's left is not a new self.
It's not a higher you.

It's just this:

Awareness.
Breath.
Stillness.
The quiet that remains
when even the one who lets go
is gone.

The Collapse of Meaning

There was a time I wanted answers.
I needed life to make sense —
not just the events,
but the timing, the pain, the purpose.

I read, I prayed, I sought wisdom.
I assigned symbols to suffering.
I gave noble names to what broke me.

And for a while, that helped.
It gave shape to chaos.
It gave the illusion of progress.
It gave me a self I could carry forward.

But meaning is a story we use
to protect ourselves from the unknown.
It comforts us.
It helps us sleep.
But it is still a veil.

The idea that everything happens *for a reason*
is the self trying to survive as interpretation.

It says:
If I can make sense of this, I can control it.

If I can name the lesson, I can find redemption.
If I can frame this pain, I don't have to sit in its silence.

Meaning becomes armor —
a beautiful distraction
from the rawness of now.

But what happens
when that story breaks?

What happens when the pain comes
and no lesson follows?

What happens when the joy comes
and it doesn't need to lead anywhere?

What happens
when nothing means anything anymore —
and you don't rush to change that?

At first, there was fear.
A subtle terror that if I gave up the search for meaning,
I would fall into nihilism.
That life would become hollow.
That nothing would matter.

But that fear belonged to the one
who needed things to matter.

The one who needed purpose
to validate existence.

And that one —
was beginning to disappear.

When meaning collapsed,
I didn't fall.
I simply stopped climbing.

The ladder dissolved.
The destination faded.
And what was left
was not absence —
but simplicity.

The burden of meaning had been so heavy.
Always trying to learn, to interpret, to transcend.
Always trying to wrestle insight out of suffering.
Always turning life into curriculum.

But when meaning collapsed,
so did the one who needed it.

Without that interpreter,
there was no more narrative.
Just this.
Just now.
Just a life happening,
with no one at the center.

It wasn't numbness.
It was peace.

Not the peace that comes from understanding —
but the peace that comes
when the need to understand
is gone.

Life continued.
I still drank tea.
I still answered messages.
I still made decisions.
But none of it needed to mean anything.

I didn't look for omens.
I didn't ask what the day was teaching me.
I didn't search for growth
in every rise and fall of emotion.

I just lived.
Present.
Unattached.
Unburdened.

And strangely —
that made everything feel more alive.

The taste of water.
The rhythm of walking.
The sound of laughter.

All free from interpretation.
All unfiltered by self.

The mind doesn't like this.
It calls it emptiness.
It calls it pointless.
It calls it lost.

Because the mind was raised on purpose.
It was taught that if something doesn't mean
something,
it's not worth living.

But awareness does not ask for meaning.
It doesn't need a story.
It doesn't need a lesson.
It only sees.

The self wants its life to be significant.
It wants to be a symbol.
A journey.
A teaching.

But the deeper truth is this:

You are not a story.
You are not a metaphor.
You are not a message waiting to be decoded.

You are simply here.

Unexplained.
Unowned.
Unfinished.
And that is enough.

The Disappearance of the Seeker

At first, I thought the path was leading somewhere.
That if I stayed faithful, if I surrendered deeply
enough,
if I listened, softened, watched…
I would arrive.

I believed there was a point to all this.

A final clearing.
A calm.
A self that was no longer in conflict.

But the longer I stayed in silence,
the more I began to sense something else:

The seeker itself —
the one doing the looking —
was beginning to fade.

Not violently.
Not suddenly.
But like fog lifting from the hills.
Like a character forgetting its lines
in the middle of the play.

The seeker is not a noble pilgrim.
It is not a true voice calling you home.
It is the echo of longing wearing the mask of purpose.

It searches not for truth —
but for continuation.

It says:
You are not yet.
There is still more to find.
And when you find it, you will finally be real.

The seeker builds the illusion
that there is someone at the center of experience
growing, evolving, arriving.

But that someone
is the very thing that prevents peace.

I tried to hold onto the practice.
Tried to observe myself.
Tried to name what was happening.

But even the one who observes
was becoming less important.
Less central.
Less necessary.

It felt like this:

I would sit in meditation
and forget to meditate.
I would breathe

and forget it was me breathing.
I would notice the silence
and then forget that I had noticed it.

And what remained
was not a better version of me.

It was **no version at all.**

There was no moment of arrival.
No summit.
No confirmation.

Just a soft unraveling
of the need to go anywhere.

The thoughts still came.
But they no longer had a destination.

Desire still moved.
But it no longer carried urgency.

The past appeared.
But it no longer told me who I was.

And without the seeker holding it all together,
the whole structure
softened.

But the seeker does not vanish without a final
disguise.

It says:
You've done it.
You've transcended.
Now stay here.
Now keep this stillness.
Now don't become like them again.

And just like that,
a new seeker is born —
now chasing spiritual security.

Even that had to go.

The urge to protect the awakening.
The pride of having seen.
The secret superiority of being the one who let go.

All of it —
just another self
trying to survive.

Eventually, even the attempt to preserve peace
was seen through.

There was nothing left to defend.
Not even stillness.
Not even silence.

I stopped trying to hold onto the moment.
I stopped trying to stay open.
I stopped trying to be here.

And what remained
was being.

The seeker is built on the promise of arrival.
It says:
There is something missing.
You must move toward it.
And one day, when you are ready, it will all make
sense.

But what if that whole structure
is made of fear?

The fear of being nothing.
The fear of not mattering.
The fear that without the journey,
there is no one there at all.

And maybe
that's the truth.

I began to see that the seeker wasn't looking for
peace.
It was looking for **itself.**

In every insight.
In every revelation.
In every book, ritual, relationship, role, teaching,
breakdown.

It was never about truth.
It was about survival.

And once I stopped feeding it —
once I stopped giving it goals,
language, context, purpose —
it simply faded.

Not with drama.
Not with grief.
But with silence.

And in that silence,
there was no one to awaken.
No one to dissolve.
No one to let go.
No one left to ask *"What's next?"*

There was no next.

Only this breath.
Only this sound.
Only this flicker of light on the wall.
Seen by no one.
Owned by no one.
Understood by no one.

Just life —
without a center.

The disappearance of the seeker
is not a loss.
It is the end of pretending
that there was ever a seeker to begin with.

What remains
is not a truth discovered.

It is a presence
that no longer needs
to become anything at all.

The Silence Beneath Thought

There is a silence
that does not begin
when the world gets quiet.

It is not the absence of sound.
It is not the gap between distractions.
It is not a state you create
by closing your eyes and breathing more slowly.

It is the silence
beneath thought.
Before thought.
After thought.

It is the ground you forgot was holding you
because your attention was always
on the flickering sky.

Most people never hear it.

Not because it isn't there,
but because the **noise of thinking** has replaced their
sense of reality.

Thought speaks constantly.
It tells you what to want.
What to fear.

What to expect.
What everything means.

It paints a world made of comparison, memory, hope,
interpretation.
A world of timelines and goals,
of narratives and shoulds,
of internal judgment posing as truth.

It is so relentless,
so familiar,
so loud in its repetition,
that it becomes the fabric of your life
without you ever seeing the weave.

But there are moments
when the fabric falls apart.

Not because you rip it —
but because something stills itself without permission.

One day, I was washing a plate.
No particular thought was on my mind.
And suddenly —
nothing.

No commentary.
No reflection.
No analysis.

Just the hand, the water, the light.
And something beneath it all

watching,
but not as a person.
More like space itself
becoming aware of its own emptiness.

There was no awe.
No bliss.
No insight.

Only a quiet
so complete
that it needed nothing to explain it.

I didn't fall into this silence
because I tried.

In fact,
all the times I tried to reach silence —
I failed.

I chased it through meditation,
through stillness,
through surrender,
through control.

I made silence the new goal.
The new self-worth.
The new proof that I was "on the path."

But every attempt to hold it
made it vanish.

Because the one trying to be silent
is the very noise
that must dissolve.

Silence is not the reward
for good spiritual behavior.
It is not the proof
that you have transcended.

It is simply
what remains
when you no longer believe
that anything must be added to this moment.

Thought does not like this silence.
It cannot survive in it.
It calls it boring.
It calls it death.
It calls it blankness.

But those are the names
thought gives to everything
it cannot control.

Because in this silence,
there is no one speaking.
No one narrating.
No one measuring or naming or managing the now.

And without that narrator,
reality returns
to its original stillness.

It does not shine.
It does not announce itself.
It does not pulse with cosmic force or radiate ecstasy.

It simply is.
Always.

Even when you were in pain.
Even when you were searching.
Even when you were chasing meaning.
The silence was there —
not waiting, not judging, not guiding —
just present.

Like a field
beneath a thousand footsteps
that never once asked who was walking.

There is a kind of listening
that does not require ears.

A kind of seeing
that does not involve the eyes.

There is a way of being
that does not begin with a thought like *"I am being
now."*

This is the silence beneath thought.
And it is not sacred.
It is not rare.
It is not special.

It is simply
the thing that has never left.

To live from this silence
is not to detach from the world.
It is to live without the one
who constantly tries to shape it.

Thoughts still come.
Sensations still arise.
The body still moves.

But it all unfolds
inside something
that does not need to understand it.

And that something
is not a self.
It is not a witness.
It is not a higher being.

It is the space
that was never born
and will never end.

The Freedom of Emptiness

There is a kind of emptiness
that is not loneliness.
Not numbness.
Not absence.

It is the kind of emptiness
you discover
when everything false has fallen away
and nothing real needs to replace it.

Not because you've lost.
But because there was never anything to hold.

At first, it felt like nothing.

Not the poetic kind.
The scary kind.
The kind that made the mind whisper:
What's the point?
What now?
Where did I go?

But slowly —
almost without noticing —
that "nothing" stopped feeling threatening.
It began to feel

like space.
Like breath.
Like freedom.

We are taught to fear emptiness.
We're taught that value must be filled —
that a life is only meaningful
if it's full of passion, people, purpose, direction.

We are also taught
that emptiness means we've disappeared.
That if we are not expressing, striving, achieving,
becoming —
we will be forgotten.
Overlooked.
Unloved.

This is the deepest myth:

That without something to offer,
you are nothing.

But the truth is this:

**You are most available to life
when you are no longer trying to be visible in it.**

Fullness can be heavy.
Fullness can be noise.
Fullness can be a mask
for a self that doesn't know how to sit still.

Emptiness is not a lack.
It is the lack of **lack**.

Nothing missing.
Nothing needed.
Nothing to prove.
Nothing to perform.

It doesn't sparkle.
It doesn't impress.
It doesn't give you anything to show.

That's why it's so free.

You don't become someone in emptiness.
You stop needing to be anyone at all.

In emptiness, there is no one left
to struggle with the moment.

No one waiting for insight.
No one resisting pain.
No one collecting experience like trophies of the soul.

Things still happen.
Tears still come.
Joy still bursts.
Grief still moves through the body.

But none of it builds a story.

There is no narrative.
Just sensation.
Then stillness.
Then whatever comes next.

But this emptiness
is not passive.

It sees.
It feels.
It knows.

Not in the way the mind knows —
through categories, through outcomes, through
identity.

This knowing is different.

It is wordless intelligence.
It does not need a name
or a conclusion.

It is a presence
so quiet
it moves without effort.

It acts
without a self.
It responds
without a goal.
It loves
without possession.

This is why emptiness is freedom:
because you are no longer doing life.
Life is doing itself —
through you,
as you,
without ever becoming *you.*

You stop trying to protect yourself.
There's no self to protect.

You stop trying to stay enlightened.
There's no light to hold.

You stop trying to stay in presence.
There's nowhere else to be.

This is not spiritual confidence.
It is not inner mastery.
It is not having the answers.

It is just **not needing anything to be different.**

Not even this.

Not even you.

The freedom of emptiness
is not a finish line.

It is the end
of the one who was racing.

And once there is no runner,
no race,
no path —
you are simply
here.

And for the first time,
it is enough.

Part III: Seeing Without a Self

There is a point on the path
where you stop walking
and realize
you were never moving.

The one who craved, resisted, searched, and questioned
has gone quiet.
And what remains
is not a person
who has become still —
but stillness itself,
watching life unfold.

You are not gone.
But you are no longer someone.

There is action,
but no actor.
There is movement,
but no mover.
There is love,
but no one trying to be good.

Everything continues,
but nothing is owned.

This is not detachment.
It is not passivity.
It is not watching from far away.

It is full presence
with no agenda.
No position.
No self-image left to defend.

You are not floating above life.
You are more in it than ever —
because you are no longer in the way.

In this part of the book,
we do not return to the world.
We never left it.

But now,
we begin to see what life looks like
when it no longer belongs to anyone.

Untethered Action

Life doesn't stop
when the self disappears.

You still answer the phone.
You still get dressed.
You still laugh, hesitate, breathe, choose.

But now,
there is no one doing it.

Action becomes light.
It rises like steam from still water —
naturally,
without intention.

There is no weight to it.
No story around it.
No one trying to control how it lands.

This is the difference:

Before, I acted to become.
To be seen.
To be consistent with the version of me I thought I
had to maintain.

Even kindness was identity.
Even silence had an audience.

But now —
the movement comes
and I move with it.

There's no rehearsal.
No explanation.
No outcome to manage.

The mind tries to claim it.
It says:
You chose that well.
You were wise.
You stayed grounded.

But there's no one here to receive that praise.
And no one here to defend against it, either.

Because the one who acted
is already gone.

There is no loss of motion.
Only the loss of ownership.

I do not act from principles.
I do not act from programming.
I do not act from some imagined inner truth.

I act
because the moment calls for action.
And when the moment is done,
there is no residue.

No aftertaste.
No pride.
No guilt.

Just movement.
Then stillness.
Then whatever comes next.

Plans still happen.
Agreements are made.
Calendars fill.

But they don't feel like strategies anymore.
They feel like outlines drawn lightly in sand.
Made in sincerity,
held without force.

There is structure —
but not tension.
Direction —
but not destiny.

I am not the planner.
I am just present
to the moment's request.

And when plans change —
as they always do —
I do not feel interrupted.

Because I was never holding anything
to begin with.

Sometimes, I move without knowing why.

A yes comes.
A no comes.
A step is taken.
A pause holds me in place.

Not from calculation.
Not from principle.
Just a quiet clarity
that doesn't explain itself.

I've learned to trust the movements
that rise when no one is asking questions.

They carry no certainty.
But they also carry no fear.

And when mistakes are made —
and they still are —
I don't have to collapse around them.

I can say:
That wasn't right.

I can apologize.
I can listen.
I can change course.

But I no longer need to protect a self.

There is no shame.
No narrative.
No identity at risk.

There is only the moment,
unfolding honestly.

Correction becomes a kind of grace.

Not a defense.
Not a punishment.
Just another breath,
adjusting to what's true now.

Untethered action
does not mean doing nothing.

It means doing what arises
without needing to be the one who does it.

Sometimes I say no.
Sometimes I make a mistake.
Sometimes I'm abrupt, or tender, or tired, or clear.

But I no longer turn it into a performance.
Or a teaching.
Or a reputation.

It happens.
It ends.
It disappears.

And I do not follow it into memory
to make it mean something.

The old way of acting
was always tied to identity.

Act like yourself.
Act your age.
Act like a good man.
Act like you know what you're doing.
Act with purpose.
Act with integrity.

But now I see:
There is no actor.
Only the action.

No role.
Only the response.

No self.
Only life,
moving through this form
as it needs to.

The Disappearance of Control

The self doesn't want peace.
It wants control.

It says it wants stillness,
but only if it can create it.
It says it wants freedom,
but only if it gets to define the terms.

It wants safety,
certainty,
advantage,
and the final say.

Even surrender can become another tactic —
another strategy to gain control
by appearing to release it.

Control doesn't always look like domination.
Sometimes it looks like preparation.
Like helpfulness.
Like calm.

It wears the face of the planner,
the perfectionist,
the peacemaker,
the healer.

It says:
I'm just trying to do this right.
I just don't want anyone to get hurt.
I just need to make sure it all goes smoothly.
I'm just being responsible.
I'm just staying centered.

But underneath every "just"
is a fear that if you don't hold it together —
you will disappear.

Control tries to manage reality
before reality can surprise you.

It tries to manage people
so you don't have to feel misunderstood.

It tries to manage your body
so you don't have to feel fragile.

It tries to manage time
so you don't have to feel the ache of impermanence.

It tries to manage your thoughts,
your voice,
your choices —
so you can stay consistent
with who you think you're supposed to be.

But every layer of control
is a layer of tension
in the nervous system.

And over time,
it becomes a prison you forgot was a performance.

But when the self dissolves,
control dissolves with it.

And what you discover
is not chaos.
Not helplessness.
Not passivity.

But flow.

Not the romantic kind.
Not the high-performance state.
Not the "alignment" the mind dreams of.

Flow that simply means
you're no longer in the way.

Life begins to move
and you stop resisting
or interpreting
or narrating
or trying to reshape it midstream.

It doesn't feel like floating.
It feels like *nothing is missing.*

Because you are no longer trying
to make the moment yours.

Plans still happen.
Choices still arise.
Things still get done.

But you are not holding them.

You are not trying to make them perfect.
You are not gripping the outcome.
You are not performing clarity.

Sometimes the plan shifts —
and you don't flinch.

Sometimes someone misunderstands —
and you don't scramble to fix it.

Sometimes you say nothing —
and the moment still unfolds.

Not because you've become passive.
But because you've stopped imagining
you are the author of reality.

And in that space —
something happens.

The breath deepens.
The shoulders soften.
The mind goes quiet.

Time feels wider.
Emotion feels softer.
Nothing feels urgent.

And in that stillness,
the body remembers something the mind never
trusted:

You were never the one in charge.
And you never needed to be.

Control never created safety.
It only created friction.

It tightened the body.
It squeezed the breath.
It filled the mind with options
and consequences
and stories of what might happen
if you let go for one second too long.

But when you stop trying to hold the world in place,
you realize
it never needed your hands to turn.

It's already turning.
With or without you.
Through you.
As you.

Letting go of control
doesn't mean letting life fall apart.

It means letting life become
what it already is
without forcing it to match
what you once needed it to be.

It means standing in the middle of uncertainty
and not folding into fear
because you remember —
there is no one to protect.

There is only this.
This breath.
This light.
This sound.
This moment.

And it is complete
without your intervention.

Relationships Without Possession

You don't stop loving
when the self dissolves.

You stop needing love
to prove that you exist.

Before, love was a mirror.
I looked for recognition.
For safety.
For someone to tell me:
You are worthy.
You are good.
You are whole.

Every interaction became a performance —
subtle, invisible, exhausting.

Even silence could be strategic.
Even presence could be proof.

I didn't love to love.
I loved to be someone
in the presence of another.

The self tries to survive
by hiding inside relationships.

It makes you the good partner.
The wise one.
The one who gives.
The one who stays.
The one who has been hurt.
The one who understands.

Even vulnerability
can be a costume.
Even spiritual intimacy
can be a negotiation.

We say: *I just want to be seen.*
But often,
we're asking:
Please reflect back to me
a version of myself I can hold onto.

But when the self disappears,
so does the need to be seen.

And suddenly,
there is so much more room
for the other person to exist.

Not as a character in your story.
Not as a mirror of your goodness.
Not as a source of approval.

Just as they are.

And that,
for the first time,
feels like love.

It's not perfect.
It's not dramatic.
It's not intoxicating.

It's simple.
Spacious.
Quiet.

You listen
without trying to fix.
You speak
without trying to impress.
You connect
without making it mean anything about you.

And when someone pulls away —
you don't chase.
Because you no longer believe
that their distance is proof
that you are lacking.

This kind of love
does not mean anything goes.

It does not mean
you abandon boundaries,
preferences,
or self-respect.

You still say no.
You still walk away.
You still tell the truth.

But the no doesn't come from pride.
The walking away doesn't come from punishment.
The truth doesn't come from the need to be right.

Clarity no longer requires conflict.
Because you are no longer trying
to win anything.

You simply let the moment
speak for itself.

There is no more possession.

Not of people.
Not of attention.
Not of memories,
stories,
roles,
or shared futures.

You can still hold someone.
But the holding is light.

They are not yours.
And you are not theirs.

You simply meet
in the moment.
And when the moment ends,
you let it go
without clinging to what it was.

And in the quiet that remains,
something deeper begins to emerge:

A love
that is not personal.

Not because it's distant —
but because it doesn't belong to anyone.

It is not about what you give
or what they return.

It is not about resonance, chemistry, agreement, or
fate.

It is simply
the movement of openness
through the space between two beings.

This love does not need to be received.
It does not need to be proven.
It does not need to survive.

It just is.

And when it's gone,
there is no grief of self-loss —
only gratitude
for what passed through.

The End of the Inner Audience

There was always someone watching.

Not outside me —
inside.
A voice.
A gaze.
A presence.

It narrated.
It corrected.
It measured.
It remembered.

And everything I did,
no matter how private,
was for its eyes.

The inner audience is the last performance.
Not for approval.
Not for survival.
Just to *be someone*
to *someone.*

It is the echo of childhood —
of being observed, judged, taught, rewarded, blamed.

It is the imprint of a life lived
in relation to mirrors.

This audience doesn't always criticize.
Sometimes it cheers you on.
It says:
You're growing.
You handled that well.
You're becoming someone wise.
This will make a great story later.
You're finally who you're supposed to be.

It smiles quietly while you speak,
watching you speak.
It applauds as you meditate,
watching you meditate.

Even in your deepest stillness,
there's still a voice whispering:
You're still.

Even when you let go,
there's someone inside
watching you let go.

I didn't realize how much I was performing
until the performance stopped.

Even the inner witness —
that gentle observer I trusted as awareness itself —
was still part of the show.

It was the final role.
The last self-image:
the one who sees.

But then,
one day,
I noticed
it wasn't there.

No applause.
No commentary.
No sense of self-monitoring.

Just walking.
Just breath.
Just dishes in the sink.
Just the silence of no one watching it happen.

And in that silence,
I didn't feel invisible.
I felt real.

This doesn't mean I lost consciousness.
It means I stopped reflecting consciousness
back at itself
like a mirror trying to admire the light.

There was no loop.
No echo.
No background recording device.

I wasn't being.
I was being.

There is an immense relief
when the inner audience is gone.

You speak — and forget what you said.
You laugh — and don't care how it sounded.
You walk into a room — and don't imagine what you
look like.

You create — and never wonder if it's good.
You connect — and don't try to be deep.
You grieve — and don't narrate your grief.

You are no longer playing
to your own idea
of who you are.

The inner audience says:
Be interesting.
Be spiritual.
Be clear.
Be strong.
Be consistent.

But freedom says:
Be nothing.
And let everything move through you.

This isn't dissociation.
It isn't detachment.
It isn't forgetting who you are.

It's the end of needing to remember
because there's no longer someone to preserve.

The moment becomes enough.
Because there is no one left
trying to keep the moment
for later.

When the inner audience disappears,
you don't feel erased.
You feel intimate with reality.

You stop watching your life happen.
And simply
let it.

Part IV: Choosing After Freedom

Nothing is left to do.
Nothing is left to become.
And yet —
life moves.

Not because you need it to mean something.
Not because you're trying to build a legacy,
prove your worth,
or fulfill a role.

But because the stillness within you
is not separate from the motion of the world.

And in that motion,
choices still appear.

Not as strategies.
Not as self-expression.
Not as identity.

But as offerings.

Small acts
not aimed at shaping your image
or securing your belonging —

but simply because they feel
true.

This part of the book is not a return
to story, self, or striving.

It is the quiet discovery
that even without identity —
there is care.
There is movement.
There is love.

And that these, too,
can be lived
without becoming anyone.

Ethics Without Identity

When the self is gone,
what guides you?

If you are not trying to be good,
not trying to be spiritual,
not trying to be respected,
what keeps you honest?

If there is no shame,
no fear of judgment,
no need to maintain consistency —
what remains
to shape your choices?

The answer is not a system.
It is not discipline.
It is not virtue.

It is something quieter.
Simpler.
Deeper.

Alignment.

Ethics without identity
is not law.
It is balance.

Not imposed from above —
but sensed from within.

Like when you're walking barefoot
and the earth tilts
and your body adjusts
without needing to think about it.

There is no reward.
No rule.
Just the intelligence of presence
moving back into coherence.

Without a self,
there is no one left to be "good."
And yet you find yourself
telling the truth anyway.
Keeping your word anyway.
Refusing to harm anyway.

Not because you're afraid of being wrong —
but because anything else
feels off in the nervous system.

Out of rhythm.
Out of tune.

You don't obey a principle.
You respond to reality.

You don't act from belief.
You act from *being*.

You don't speak up to be brave.
You don't stay quiet to be wise.
You don't walk away to be righteous.

These things happen
because they feel whole
in the moment.

And when the moment passes,
you don't replay it
to confirm you were right.

There's no audience.
No scoreboard.
No journal entry waiting to be written.

Just a breath.
Then the next one.
Then the next.

But ethics without identity
does not mean passivity.
It doesn't mean nothing matters.
It doesn't mean you float above conflict
and let the world fall apart.

You can still take a stand.
You can still say no.
You can still feel outrage,

grief,
urgency.

But there is no image of the "just one"
or the "compassionate one"
performing it.

You are not trying to be the person
who protects or confronts.

You are simply the space
through which truth moves
when it's needed.

Sometimes that truth looks fierce.
Sometimes it looks soft.
Sometimes it is silence.
Sometimes it is leaving.
Sometimes it is staying.

But always —
it arises cleanly.
Not to prove.
Not to win.
Not to be seen.

Just because
anything else
would not feel real.

This is how ethics survives
the disappearance of self.

Not as duty.
Not as virtue.
But as clarity
without commentary.

As movement
without performance.

As care
without costume.

Purpose Without Persona

You don't need a persona
to live with purpose.

You don't need a mission statement
to offer something real.

You don't need to believe in your path
to walk it.

Purpose is not found.
It is not chosen.
It is not declared.

It is revealed
when you stop trying to be someone
and start listening to what moves through you
when you are no longer performing.

Before, purpose was identity.

It said:
I am here to serve.
I am a healer.
I am a guide.
I am a creator.
I am here to help people see something.

Even the noblest intentions
were wrapped in self-image.

We didn't just live with purpose —
we *became* it.
We wore it like a name.
We fed it with meaning.
We turned it into a stage.

But when the persona dissolves,
you discover that purpose does not end.
It simply loses its costume.

You might still teach.
Still build.
Still serve.
Still lead.

But it does not feel like becoming.
It feels like being used
by something larger
that does not need your name
on the end of it.

There is a kind of action
that doesn't ask:
What am I called to do?
It simply arises
because nothing in you resists doing it.

There is no plan.
No branding.
No audience.
Just the next quiet yes.

You paint.
Not to be an artist —
but because something beautiful moved through your
hands.

You speak.
Not to build a platform —
but because something clear asked to be voiced.

You serve.
Not to be good —
but because compassion moved
before the mind had time to narrate it.

You build.
Then let go.
Then build again.
Without trying to leave a mark.

Because the work was never yours to hold.

Purpose without persona
has no shape to maintain.

Some days it's fierce.
Some days it's invisible.
Some days it leaves no trace at all.

And that's the freedom of it:

There is no longer a "you"
who needs to justify your direction
or prove your usefulness.

There is only presence,
offering itself
where it's most needed —
then letting go.

Some purposes stay for years.
Some visit for an afternoon.

None of them need to be *you.*
None of them need to be framed as *destiny.*

They do not ask to be remembered.
Only to be answered.

And when they are done,
they release you
with the same silence
they arrived in.

The Lightness of Participation

You don't have to disappear
to be free.

You can still dance.
Still speak.
Still build.
Still join the world
in its mess, its rhythm, its ache.

You are not separate.
You are not beyond it.
You are not above it.

You are simply
no longer confused by it.

Participation without self
feels different.

You no longer enter rooms
trying to be someone.

You no longer join conversations
trying to be right
or deep
or useful.

You don't perform presence.
You don't scan for impact.
You don't listen for applause.

You simply show up
because you're already here.

The body moves.
The voice responds.
The hands create.
The eyes soften.

And it all happens
without effort,
without plan,
without image.

It feels like breath.
Not noise.
Not spotlight.
Not proof.

Just breath.

You laugh now
without worrying how it lands.
You speak now
without shaping how it sounds.
You lead now
without needing anyone to follow.

You don't hide from visibility.
You don't cling to it either.
You just let the moment decide
how loud or quiet you are.

Some days you are called to whisper.
Some days you are asked to roar.

Neither makes you more real.

The self once made every act heavy.
A performance to maintain.
A persona to confirm.
A moment to package for meaning.

But now you notice
what's missing:

No monologue.
No measuring.
No second-guessing.
No story being built
out of every interaction.

Just presence,
responding.

You still say the wrong thing sometimes.
You still trip over your words.
You still miss the moment.

But none of it gets stored
in your identity.

There is no residue.
No guilt.
No pride.
No image to edit.

Just life,
widening,
moving,
vanishing.

Participation becomes
not a duty,
not a mission,
but an offering
made by the moment
to itself.

And you,
freed from the burden of being anyone,
get to enjoy it.

Like a breeze
that arrives without reason.
Like a child
who plays without audience.

Like life
returning to itself
in full lightness.

The Sacred in the Seemingly Ordinary

The miracle is not awakening.
It's making tea
with nothing in the way.

You don't need revelations anymore.
You don't need cosmic clarity.
You don't need insight
to justify your breath.

You wash the dishes.
And it is enough.

You walk to the door.
And it is enough.

You fold the towel,
sip the soup,
water the plant.

And each one
is complete.

There is no grand truth left to carry.
No state to protect.
No secret knowing to preserve.

Just this moment —
this completely unspecial moment —
arriving fully,
without needing to become anything else.

The sacred is not found in stillness.
It is the stillness.

It is not hidden in beauty.
It is what allows beauty
to pass through
without being held.

It does not deepen in grief.
It is what allows grief to unfold
without needing to mean anything.

You still cry.
But now the crying doesn't shape a story.
It doesn't build a self.
It doesn't need to be processed.

It moves.
And then it doesn't.

And you are still here.

You still notice beauty.
But you don't try to keep it.

The way a leaf falls in the sunlight.
The sound of birds at 4 a.m.
The way someone says your name
without even knowing
they've touched you.

You don't try to name it.
You don't try to share it.
You just let it pass
through the body
like breath.

The sacred is not rare.
It is not elevated.
It is not earned.

It is the sound of your spoon
against the side of a bowl.

It is the way your socks
land near the bed.

It is the quiet before a sentence.
The way the light bends
before it disappears.

It is the soft ache
in the chest
when nothing needs to happen next.

You don't need to look for signs.
You don't need to ask what it means.

The smell of toast is enough.
The hum of the fridge is enough.
The pause in traffic is enough.
The breath before sleep
is enough.

Because you are no longer the one
measuring what matters.

The sacred is not hidden.
It was never hidden.

It was simply obscured
by the self that needed something more.

Now that self is gone.
And all that remains
is what was here the whole time.

Unnamed.
Unclaimed.
Undisturbed.

The End of Becoming

No more steps.
No more roles.
No more one who needs to be free.

The story has ended —
not in triumph,
not in collapse —
but in the simple absence
of the one who needed a story.

The quiet doesn't grow louder.
It doesn't change color.
It doesn't bloom into some greater truth.

It just stays —
unclaimed,
unimpressed,
unfolding
without anyone left
to measure it.

The fire did not consume you.
It consumed the costume.
It consumed the audience.
It consumed the stage.

And what remains now
was never burning.

You are not what lived through the fire.
You are what was never touched by it.

The life that remains
is not yours.

It is life —
moving,
breathing,
disappearing —
without a name
to hold it.

You are not here to perform your light.
You are the light —
even when it's dark.

You don't need to shine.
You don't need to prove.
You don't need to hold your pose.

You just need to be so free
that even your story
lets go of you.

Let others chase the idea of arrival.
Let them build temples out of certainty.

You know better now.

You know the sacred wears no crown.
You know truth never needs a defense.
You know freedom doesn't shout.

It just breathes.

And here you are.
Breathing.

Without answers.
Without armor.
Without agenda.

Just life —
undressed,

undivided,
undeniably yours.

The fire didn't destroy you.
It revealed
that you were never burning.

Only the costume was.

www.ingramcontent.com/pod-product-compliance
Lightning Source LLC
Chambersburg PA
CBHW021117130626
46554CB00002B/745